healing rain

MICHAEL W. SMITH

WITH WENDY LEE NENTWIG

INTEGRITY®
PUBLISHERS
Nashville

...I will send down

showers in season,

there will be

showers of blessing.

— EZEKIEL 34:26B

Songwriting is an interesting process. Sometimes it's a struggle to get the words and music on paper, and other songs seem like they're just waiting to be written. "Healing Rain" falls into the second category. The music came to me in five minutes, and it was still in my head when I sat down in my Franklin studio with Martin Smith to write. Within about thirty minutes he had the finished song, using me as a sounding board for the lyrics.

Not that there weren't detours along the way.

Originally, I thought it would be called "Healing Train." The theme of healing and restoration was the same, but in my mind, I imagined this train coming to town loaded down with medical supplies, providing help and healing for people with all different kinds of diseases. I saw the song as a metaphor for the spiritual healing God wants to bring to each of us.

In the end, the change wasn't such a huge shift. The song is still inspired by the hurting people I encounter at my concerts. Night after night I hear stories of pain and heartbreak, loss and suffering. And while each tale is unique, what I want to tell each person is the same: It may be hard to believe right now, but God is still in the business of restoring people's lives. And you know what? He's really good at it.

This isn't just something I say to make them (and myself) feel better for a minute or two. I see God at work in people's lives every day, restoring them emotionally, spiritually and physically. He wants to do the same for us. All we need to do is ask, because God is waiting with a second chance, with open arms, with forgiveness.

He's ready and willing. He wants to wash each of us clean . . . in His healing rain.

Are you ready?

—*Michael W. Smith*

Life, like the weather, can be unpredictable.

One minute the sky is clear and blue; the next, a storm has you running for cover. Sickness, loss, heartbreak . . . they can quickly turn life's blue skies to gray. But God is with us in the rain as well as the sunshine. In fact, it's often during those overcast days that we see our heavenly Father most clearly. Along the way, we also tend to learn a little something about ourselves and just what we're made of.

While we might find ourselves regularly wishing for sunshine, if we put our trust in Him, we'll be ready for whatever the day brings.

healing rain

IS COMING DOWN

IT'S COMING NEARER

TO THIS OLD TOWN

rich and poor

WEAK AND STRONG

IT'S BRINGING MERCY

IT WON'T BE LONG

"For I know the plans I have for you," *declares the* LORD. *"Plans to prosper you and not to harm you, plans to give you hope and a future."*

Sorrow looks back,

worry looks around,

faith looks up.

— RALPH WALDO EMERSON

In case you've ever found yourself thinking, *God couldn't possibly care about someone like me,* you should know that He sent His Son for all of us. Rich or poor, weak or strong,

His mercy and grace are waiting for each of us.

Isn't it wonderful to know we serve an equal-opportunity Savior?

Consider how the lilies grow. They do not labor or spin. Yet I tell you, not even Solomon in all his splendor was dressed like one of these. If that is how God clothes the grass of the field, which is here today and tomorrow is thrown into the fire, how much more will he clothe you, O you of little faith!

—LUKE 12:27-29

healing rain

IS COMING DOWN

IT'S COMING CLOSER

TO THE LOST AND FOUND

tears of joy

AND TEARS OF SHAME

ARE WASHED FOREVER

IN JESUS' NAME

Because of the LORD's great love

we are not consumed,

for his compassions never fail.

They are new every morning . . .

— LAMENTATIONS 3:22-23A

God is less concerned

with where you've been

than with where you're going.

We have all probably wished at one time or another that we could hit life's "rewind" button to undo some hurtful act or poor choice. The prodigal son was very familiar with that feeling of regret.

He was given his inheritance early and threw it away on parties and frivolous fun. When he finally returned home, hungry and ashamed, he was simply hoping to be hired on as a servant. But before he could even reach the house, his father came running to greet him.

What was lost had been found.

God feels that way about us. Even though we wander off again and again, He is waiting for us to turn toward home. And as soon as we do, He'll be running out to meet us.

Sow for yourselves righteousness,

reap the fruit of unfailing love . . .

for it is time to seek the LORD,

until he comes and

showers righteousness on you.

— HOSEA 10:12

healing rain

IT COMES WITH FIRE

SO LET IT FALL

AND TAKE US HIGHER

healing rain

I'M NOT AFRAID

TO BE WASHED

IN HEAVEN'S RAIN

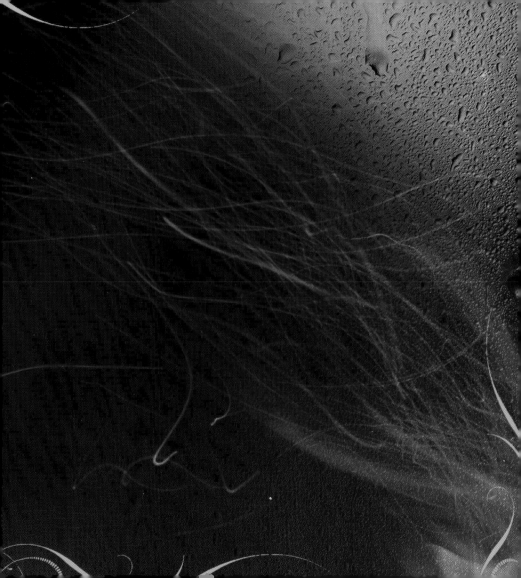

But the eyes of the LORD are on those

who fear him, on those whose

hope is in his unfailing love.

— PSALM 33:18

Some of us are so busy

being sick,

we don't have time

to get well.

The unknown can be scary

even when God is leading the way.

We say we want to change—to give the Lord control of our lives—but it's not easy trading what we think we want for *what* He knows we *need.*

It requires not just believing that He really is who He says, but living like it as well.

Things do not change,
we do.

—HENRY DAVID THOREAU

lift your heads

LET US RETURN

TO THE MERCY SEAT

WHERE TIME BEGAN

AND IN YOUR EYES

I see the pain

COME SOAK THIS DRY HEART

WITH HEALING RAIN

The LORD is my light and my salvation—

whom shall I fear? The LORD is the stronghold

of my life—of whom shall I be afraid?

— PSALM 27:1

Often, the best place to start is at the beginning.

These days, when we find ourselves in need of help, we turn in a lot of different directions: to friends, books, counselors . . . everywhere but God.

Help is just a prayer away

and yet we forget to go there first. We're so anxious to reach the end of a problem that we try to skip ahead. But we never save ourselves time or trouble by leaving God out of our lives.

Love comforts like

sunshine after the rain.

— WILLIAM SHAKESPEARE

and only You

THE SON OF MAN

CAN TAKE A LEPER

AND LET HIM STAND

so lift your hands

THEY CAN BE HELD

BY SOMEONE GREATER

THE GREAT I AM

. . . He said to the paralytic, "I tell you, get up, take your mat and go home." He got up, took his mat and walked out in full view of them all. This amazed everyone and they praised God, saying, "We have never seen anything like this."

— MARK 2:10b-12

let God be God

Sometimes it's easy to think

God needs our help—

a little nudge in the right direction.

But we forget that we're dealing with

the Creator of the universe.

"*Where were you when I laid the earth's foundation? Tell me, if you understand, who marked off its dimensions? Surely you know! Who stretched a measuring line across it? On what were its footings set, or who laid this cornerstone—while the morning stars sang together and all the angels shouted for joy?*"

—JOB 38:4-7

HE . . . SENDS RAIN ON THE RIGHTEOUS AND THE UNRIGHTEOUS.

MATTHEW 5:45B

He saved us through the washing of rebirth

and renewal by the Holy Spirit.

TITUS 3:5

"*I will send rain on the land.*"

1 KINGS 18:1

. . . UNTIL HE COMES AND
SHOWERS RIGHTEOUSNESS ON YOU.

HOSEA 10:12

. . . wash me, and I will be whiter than snow.

PSALM 51:7

. . . the spring of living water . . .

JEREMIAH 2:13

"I BAPTIZE YOU WITH WATER . . ."

MATTHEW 3:11

wash away all my iniquity

and cleanse me . . .

PSALM 51:2

and rain fell on the earth forty days and forty nights . . .

GENESIS 7:12

AS A NORTH WIND BRINGS RAIN . . .

PROVERBS 25:23

water

References to it are found throughout the Old and New Testaments. From the Creation story to the great flood to Jesus turning it into wine, water signified either new life, or death—or the miraculous power of Christ.

In our lives today, we can still see water at work. When a summer rainstorm leaves our world seeming fresh and clean. When floodwaters wreak havoc and cost lives. When we witness a baptism and are left marveling at the life-changing power of God.

But water has no power outside of God. So when I sing about healing rain, I'm not thinking about storms or raindrops. I'm calling on the true Source of all healing. I hope you recognize Him in my music and have made Him part of your life as well.

I know God won't give me

anything I can't handle.

I just wish He didn't

trust me so much.

— MOTHER TERESA

"Come to me, all you who are

weary and burdened, and

I will give you rest."

— MATTHEW 11:28

Restore us,

O God.

Healing Rain

Written by Michael W. Smith,

Martin Smith and Matt Bronleewe

healing rain

IS COMING DOWN

IT'S COMING NEARER

TO THIS OLD TOWN

RICH AND POOR

WEAK AND STRONG

IT'S BRINGING MERCY

IT WON'T BE LONG

healing rain

IS COMING DOWN

IT'S COMING CLOSER

TO THE LOST AND FOUND

TEARS OF JOY

AND TEARS OF SHAME

ARE WASHED FOREVER

IN JESUS' NAME

healing rain

IT COMES WITH FIRE

SO LET IT FALL

AND TAKE US HIGHER

HEALING RAIN

I'M NOT AFRAID

TO BE WASHED

IN HEAVEN'S RAIN

LIFT YOUR HEADS

LET US RETURN

TO THE MERCY SEAT

WHERE TIME BEGAN

AND IN YOUR EYES

I SEE THE PAIN

COME SOAK THIS DRY HEART

with healing rain

AND ONLY YOU

THE SON OF MAN

CAN TAKE A LEPER

AND LET HIM STAND

SO LIFT YOUR HANDS

THEY CAN BE HELD

BY SOMEONE GREATER

THE GREAT I AM

healing rain

IT COMES WITH FIRE

SO LET IT FALL

AND TAKE US HIGHER

healing rain

I'M NOT AFRAID

TO BE WASHED

IN HEAVEN'S RAIN

TO BE WASHED IN HEAVEN'S RAIN

healing rain

IS FALLING DOWN

healing rain

IS FALLING DOWN

I'M NOT AFRAID

I'M NOT AFRAID

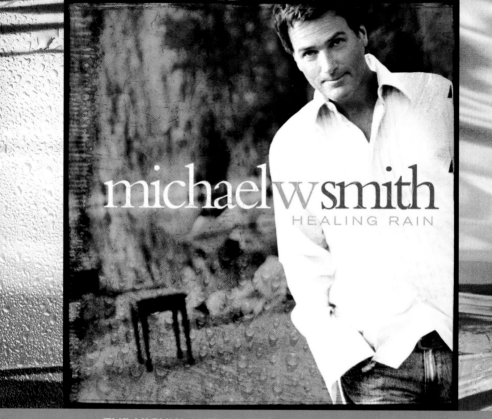

michael w smith
HEALING RAIN

THE HIGHLY ANTICIPATED NEW STUDIO ALBUM
AVAILABLE NOW
WHEREVER GREAT MUSIC IS SOLD.

See Michael on tour in a city near you!
For tour information, visit:
www.michaelwsmith.com • www.reunionrecords.com

provident
LABEL GROUP

reunion records